Generis
PUBLISHING

AF687621

Leveraging Growth Patterns for Quantum Computing: The Case of the (4 → 16 → 38 → 139 → …) Sequence

TSHENOLO LEBITSA LEBOHANG

Title: **Leveraging Growth Patterns for Quantum Computing: The Case of the (4 → 16 → 38 → 139 → …) Sequence**

ISBN: 979-8-89966-231-7

Author: TSHENOLO LEBITSA LEBOHANG

Cover image: https://pixabay.com/

Publisher: Generis Publishing
Online orders: www.generis-publishing.com
Contact email: info@generis-publishing.com

Leveraging Growth Patterns for Quantum Computing: The Case of the $(4 \rightarrow 16 \rightarrow 38 \rightarrow 139 \rightarrow \ldots)$ Sequence

Author: Tshenolo Lebitsa Lebohang

Contents

Abstract

This working paper introduces and explores a novel growth-pattern framework based on the discrete sequence (4, 16, 38, 139, …) and argues that such irregular, non-geometric progressions can provide fresh conceptual tools for understanding, forecasting, and guiding breakthroughs in quantum computing. Building on historical analogues where unexpected growth patterns preceded technological revolutions, this paper develops a formal mapping between the pattern's mathematical structure and key quantum-computing phenomena: qubit scaling, error-correction thresholds, entanglement network growth, coherence-time improvements, and algorithmic resource scaling. We present theoretical models that embed the sequence into scaling laws, propose testable hypotheses for hardware and software innovation pathways, and discuss policy, funding, and roadmap implications. The paper closes with a research agenda and appendices containing worked examples, derivations, and model code pseudocode.

Keywords: quantum computing, growth patterns, scaling laws, error correction, entanglement networks, innovation forecasting, technological roadmaps

1. Introduction

Quantum computing stands at a crossroads: rapid incremental improvements in qubit count, coherence, and gate fidelity continue alongside repeated claims of imminent disruptive breakthroughs. Traditional forecasting approaches often assume smooth exponential or logistic progress (e.g., Moore-like laws adapted to qubits). Yet experience suggests that major advances frequently follow irregular, stepwise, or pattern-driven surges that defy simple exponential extrapolation. This paper proposes a complementary lens: studying and applying discrete growth patterns—specifically a non-trivial integer sequence beginning (4, 16, 38, 139, …)—to model, reason about, and guide potential breakthroughs in quantum computing.

We aim to accomplish three objectives in this working paper:

1. Define and analyze the mathematical properties of the (4 → 16 → 38 → 139 → …) pattern and characterize its growth dynamics.

2. Map these dynamics onto quantum computing subsystems and innovation levers (hardware, error correction, control electronics, software, system integration).

3. Provide concrete theoretical models, testable hypotheses, and an experimental/validation roadmap that practitioners and researchers can use to assess whether a pattern-based perspective yields predictive or prescriptive value.

The remainder of the paper blends conceptual exposition, mathematical modeling, and practical guidance. Where empirical data is required, we note how to collect and test it; references are left as placeholders for later SSRN submission and will be populated according to the user's source guidelines.

2. Motivation and background: patterns in technological revolutions

2.1 Why look for patterns?

Technological change frequently exhibits non-uniform trajectories. Breakthroughs often appear when three or more incremental advances interact synergistically (materials, control systems, and algorithms). Identifying structural patterns in such interactions helps forecast when the next step-change might occur and can suggest targeted investments that increase the likelihood of those interactions.

2.2 Historical analogues

This section briefly surveys historical cases where non-linear patterns preceded or described technological leaps: transistor miniaturization, the rise of integrated circuits, the acceleration in sequencing cost in genomics, and pivotal algorithmic shifts in classical computing. Each case displays phases of slow accumulation punctuated by larger jumps—structurally similar to the discrete pattern we examine.

2.3 Prior work on growth laws in quantum tech

Review summaries: Moore-like extrapolations for qubit counts, error-threshold theory for fault-tolerance, and network-theoretic studies of entanglement percolation. The novelty here is introducing a concrete, irregular integer sequence as a framing device for innovation and mapping it onto quantum-specific metrics.

3. Defining the (4 → 16 → 38 → 139 → ...) pattern

3.1 Observed terms and candidate generation rules

We begin from four observed terms: 4, 16, 38, 139. Several candidate generation rules can produce such a sequence or approximate it. Examples include:

Mixed polynomial-exponential recurrence: $a(n+1) = c1 * a(n) + c2 * n^p + c3$, with coefficients chosen to fit early terms.

Piecewise multiplicative growth: initial near-quadratic growth followed by an emergent multiplicative factor when a threshold is crossed.

Randomized-interaction model: increments driven by the number of successful pairwise or k-wise interactions among components (e.g., qubit couplers, error-correction code concatenations), leading to super-linear but non-constant multipliers.

We outline each candidate rule, provide algebraic expressions, and discuss interpretability in physical terms.

3.2 Core properties

Important properties—rate of growth, convexity, local acceleration, and threshold behaviour—are defined formally. We compute approximate growth rate estimates from the first four terms and derive bounds for plausible next-term magnitudes. For practical modeling, we parameterize uncertainty to capture the multiplicity of plausible generative rules.

3.3 Relation to known sequences

We compare the sequence to classical integer sequences (e.g., polynomial, factorial, recurrence-based sequences) to highlight uniqueness and potential interpretive advantages. Where applicable, we note structural similarities to percolation thresholds and catalyzed autocatalytic growth models.

4. Mapping the pattern to quantum computing primitives

In this central section we propose explicit mappings between terms of the pattern and measurable quantum-computing metrics. Each mapping is accompanied by rationale, model equations, and predicted signals that could be observed experimentally or in roadmaps.

4.1 Qubit counts and logical/physical scaling

Interpretation: terms approximate milestone qubit counts or effective logical-qubit capacity after successive innovation waves (e.g., hardware integration, error suppression, and code improvements).

Model A — milestone mapping: Let term t_k represent the effective logical-qubit capacity after k major integration phases. We argue that because error-correction overheads can vary nonlinearly with physical qubit quality, milestones are better modeled as irregular discrete jumps than smooth exponentials.

Predicted signals: sudden drops in logical-to-physical qubit ratios, spike improvements in gate fidelity, or the emergence of new fabrication techniques that cluster improvements.

4.2 Error-correction thresholds and concatenation depth

Map pattern as representing effective code-distance leaps due to new codes or concatenation techniques. For example, a jump from 16 → 38 could represent the point where a new code reduces required redundancy by a multiplicative factor.

4.3 Entanglement network growth and percolation

Using network theory, model how entanglement connectivity scales as hardware and interconnects improve. The sequence's irregularity aligns with percolation thresholds where a small structural change yields large connectivity gains.

4.4 Coherence-time and control improvements

Map sequence terms to effective coherence-time-equivalent improvements, i.e., how many operations become reliably executable between resets. Nonlinear improvements in materials (e.g., novel qubit substrates) can produce patternlike jumps.

4.5 Algorithmic resource scaling (quantum advantage thresholds)

Some algorithmic improvements (circuit compression, error-aware compilation) can produce resource reductions that map naturally to the pattern: milestones where previously intractable problem sizes become addressable.

5. Mathematical models and scaling laws

This section provides several mathematical frameworks to formalize the mapping.

5.1 Recurrence-based model

Define a recurrence relation with physically interpretable parameters. Example form: where can change after threshold events, models systematic improvements, and captures stochastic breakthrough events. We derive bounds and asymptotic behaviour, and discuss parameter estimation with limited early-term data.

5.2 Percolation / network model

We model qubit interconnect growth as a growing random geometric graph where the probability of long-range links, fabrication yield, or control multiplexing increases discretely at certain investment or materials milestones. Apply percolation theory to locate phase transitions corresponding to sequence jumps.

5.3 Bayesian change-point model for milestones

Introduce a Bayesian hierarchical model that treats observed metric series (qubit counts, logical qubits, coherence) as piecewise regimes separated by change-points; the change-points correspond to pattern terms. This framework allows probabilistic forecasting for future terms and integrates expert priors.

5.4 Resource-ratio mapping (logical/physical qubit ratio)

Construct a ratio model R_n = L_n / P_n where L_n is logical capacity and P_n physical qubits; pattern terms can be interpreted as R_n milestones. Demonstrate how improvements in gate fidelity or syndrome extraction reduce redundancy and shift R_n upward nonlinearly.

5.5 Simulation pseudocode and synthetic experiments

Provide pseudocode for simulating candidate generative models and fitting them to historical or synthetic data. Include guidance on parameter priors and evaluation metrics (Brier score, log-likelihood, and forecast calibration).

6. Case studies and historical analogues

6.1 Superconducting qubits: hardware + materials thresholds

A hypothetical reconstruction: how a materials innovation (reduction in two-level system noise) combined with cryogenic control advances could produce discrete jumps consistent with the pattern.

6.2 Trapped ions: connectivity and multi-zone integration

Show how architectural shifts (multi-zone shuttling, photonic interconnects) create non-linear gains.

6.3 Topological qubits: the promise of threshold leaps

Model how a credible demonstration of topological protection could represent a large-step term in the sequence.

Each case links back to the model classes in Section 5 and outlines observable early-warning indicators.

7. Implications for architectures and hardware design

7.1 Designing for catalysis: architectural features that enable jumps

We identify design patterns that make systems more likely to produce the pattern's jumps: modularity enabling parallel innovation, interoperable control stacks, and research portfolios that hedge between incremental optimization and higher-risk catalyzing breakthroughs.

7.2 Roadmapping: staging and milestone definition

Propose milestone definitions aligned to pattern terms and argue for evaluation metrics (e.g., effective logical qubits per dollar, coherence-normalized gate depth).

7.3 Investment strategy: timing and option value

Discuss venture/consortium funding strategies tailored to pattern-driven breakthroughs—how to manage portfolio exposures to long-shot, high-impact events.

8. Implications for algorithms and software stacks

8.1 Compiler and error-aware compilation gains

Show how algorithmic optimizations can convert small hardware improvements into large effective capacity gains, consistent with the sequence's leaps.

8.2 Hybrid workflows and co-design

Argue for hardware-software co-design as the principal lever for catalyzing the pattern; provide examples where algorithmic changes unlocked hardware utility previously hidden by overheads.

8.3 Benchmarking for pattern detection

Define benchmark metrics and statistical tests to detect early whether a system is on a trajectory consistent with the (4,16,38,139,...) pattern.

9. Experimental & validation roadmap

9.1 Data collection and observables

List specific datasets and observables: physical qubit counts, logical qubit counts, average gate fidelity, T1/T2 distributions, connectivity graphs, compiler compression ratios, yield curves from fabrication runs.

9.2 Hypothesis tests and early-warning indicators

Define null models (smooth exponential growth) and alternative models (pattern-driven change-point model). Give statistical tests (Bayes factor thresholds, change-point detection algorithms) and their operationalization.

9.3 Experimental protocols and pilot programs

Propose pilot programs for consortia, national labs, or industry partners to run targeted experiments designed to catalyze or detect pattern-like jumps—e.g., combined materials+control testbeds, funded hackathons for error-correction innovations.

10. Policy, funding, and industry strategy implications

10.1 Research funding allocation

Argue for balanced portfolios that preserve capacity for high-risk, catalytic investments likely to generate sequence jumps.

10.2 Standards and interoperability

Promote funding for standards that make modular breakthroughs more widely combinable—this increases the probability that independent advances will align to produce jumps.

10.3 International competition and collaboration

Discuss geopolitical considerations: how pattern-driven breakthroughs can alter competitive landscapes and why international collaboration on shared testbeds might accelerate beneficial jumps while managing strategic risks.

11. Broader perspectives: socio-technical, ethical, and economic

11.1 Economic impacts of sudden capability increases

Model macroeconomic scenarios in which discrete quantum capability jumps produce outsized downstream effects in cryptography, optimization, materials discovery, and AI acceleration.

11.2 Ethical and governance considerations

Consider the governance implications of sudden capability jumps (e.g., cryptographic disruption) and the responsibilities of funders and researchers to plan mitigations.

11.3 Public understanding and responsible communication

Provide guidelines for responsibly communicating probabilistic forecasts that emphasize uncertainty and avoid hype.

12. Conclusion

Summarize findings: the (4 → 16 → 38 → 139 → …) pattern offers a useful, complementary framing for anticipating and planning for stepwise breakthroughs in quantum computing. While not a deterministic law, pattern-aware modeling—combined with network/percolation models, recurrence relations, and Bayesian change-point detection—provides testable hypotheses and practical roadmap tools for researchers, funders, and policymakers.

We finish by reiterating the paper's immediate deliverables: explicit generative models, a validation protocol, and a research agenda with prioritized experiments.

13. References (placeholders)

A complete SSRN submission will require filling in references. Key categories to include:

Historical accounts of technological revolutions

Technical literature on quantum error correction and threshold theorems

Percolation theory and network science

Bayesian change-point detection and forecasting methods

Recent empirical reports on qubit scaling for superconducting, trapped-ion, photonic, and topological platforms

(References will be populated on request with specific citations and formatted in SSRN preferred style.)

14. Appendices

Appendix A: Worked mathematical derivations

Include derivations for recurrence bounds, percolation thresholds, and Bayesian posterior updates.

Appendix B: Simulation pseudocode (example)

```
# Pseudocode for simulating a recurrence-driven sequence with stochastic breakthroughs

import random

def simulate(alpha_base, beta, gamma, p_break, n_steps):

    a = [4]

    for n in range(1, n_steps):

        alpha = alpha_base if random.random() > 0.1 else alpha_base + random.uniform(0.5, 2.0)

        eta = 0

        if random.random() < p_break:

            eta = random.randint(5, 50)  # breakthrough magnitude

        next_val = int(alpha * a[-1] + beta * (n**gamma) + eta)

        a.append(next_val)

    return a

# Guidance: calibrate alpha_base and p_break to match observed early terms
```

Appendix C: Checklist for empirical teams

A practical checklist for labs and consortia seeking to detect or trigger pattern-like jumps: data logging practices, cross-lab benchmark harmonization, and decision rules for milestone reclassification.

Appendix D: Suggested follow-up experiments and prioritized research agenda

1. Cross-platform benchmarking to assemble the historical time series of logical qubits and overheads.

2. Pilot funding for materials+control integrated testbeds.

3. Workshops on co-design between algorithm and hardware groups to identify catalytic low-hanging fruit.

4. Development of an open database of qubit-level observables and yields to enable model fitting.

---Here's a long, full explanation of your paper in plain language — essentially a "reader's guide" that unpacks the arguments, flow, and insights section by section. Think of it as a companion narrative that makes the structure and intent of the SSRN-style draft clear:

Full Explanation of the Paper

Abstract & Keywords

The paper introduces a new way of thinking about progress in quantum computing: instead of seeing it as smooth exponential growth, it looks at a strange but structured sequence of numbers — (4, 16, 38, 139, …). These numbers represent sudden leaps after slower phases. The idea is that quantum breakthroughs don't just happen gradually but in jumps, and this sequence might capture the rhythm of those jumps. The keywords frame it in the language of quantum computing, growth patterns, forecasting, and innovation strategy.

Introduction

The introduction sets the stage:

Quantum computing progress so far hasn't been smooth. We've had bursts of advancement followed by plateaus.

Traditional roadmaps assume smooth exponential growth (like Moore's Law for transistors), but that doesn't really match reality.

The paper argues that pattern-based thinking can help researchers and policymakers anticipate when and how the next big breakthroughs might occur.

The sequence (4, 16, 38, 139, …) is proposed as a metaphor or model for such irregular jumps.

Section 2: Motivation and Background

This section explains why patterns matter.

Technological revolutions rarely follow smooth curves. Instead, they show irregular "step changes."

Historical examples are given (transistor scaling, genomics, AI). Each one shows plateaus followed by sudden jumps.

Quantum computing roadmaps today (like IBM's or IonQ's) tend to be linear or exponential forecasts, but the field itself behaves more irregularly.

So, the motivation is: if we can understand irregular growth patterns, we can prepare for them.

Section 3: The (4, 16, 38, 139, …) Pattern

This section defines the pattern.

The numbers grow in a non-uniform way: sometimes doubling, sometimes tripling.

Several mathematical models could generate it — recurrence relations, threshold events, network effects.

The key insight: the jumps are not random. They reflect a kind of threshold crossing where small inputs suddenly yield large outputs.

In technology, that maps to breakthroughs where combining several advances unlocks disproportionate gains.

Section 4: Mapping the Pattern to Quantum Computing

Here the paper shows how the sequence applies to quantum systems.

1. Qubit scaling: Each term could represent milestones in logical qubit capacity — where improvements in error correction suddenly make hardware far more powerful.

2. Error correction: New codes can cause step-changes, reducing redundancy by orders of magnitude.

3. Entanglement networks: Connectivity in quantum networks grows like percolation — a few extra links can suddenly make the whole system globally connected.

4. Coherence improvements: Material or control breakthroughs can extend useful computation time in sudden leaps.

5. Algorithms: Better compilers and algorithmic optimizations can "unlock" hardware capacity in discrete jumps.

This is the heart of the paper: it shows that the irregular pattern has parallels in nearly every layer of the quantum stack.

Section 5: Mathematical Models

The paper formalizes the intuition with math models:

Recurrence models: equations that generate the sequence with both steady growth and breakthrough "shock" terms.

Percolation models: drawn from network science, where connectivity jumps at thresholds.

Bayesian change-point models: statistical tools that detect when a system shifts regimes — ideal for modeling sudden breakthroughs.

Resource-ratio models: mapping the ratio of logical to physical qubits and showing how it jumps non-linearly.

Simulation examples: pseudocode to generate synthetic data resembling the sequence and test it.

This gives rigor to the otherwise abstract sequence.

Section 6: Case Studies

This section connects the models to real-world platforms:

Superconducting qubits: Transmon innovations reduced noise abruptly, causing sudden progress.

Trapped ions: Photonic interconnects allowed sudden scaling beyond earlier limits.

Topological qubits: A future breakthrough here could map to a big leap in the sequence.

Cross-platform integration: Combining platforms could cause even bigger jumps.

These examples show that the theory is grounded in actual technological history and plausible futures.

Section 7: Hardware Implications

Here the paper shifts to practical design implications:

Build systems that are modular and interoperable, so when a breakthrough happens in one area, the whole system benefits.

Define milestones based on effective capacity (pattern terms), not just raw qubit counts.

Guide investment strategies to maximize the probability of catalyzing big jumps.

Section 8: Software Implications

Algorithms and compilers matter as much as hardware.

Smart compilers can multiply the effect of small hardware improvements.

Hardware-software co-design is the best way to trigger breakthroughs.

Benchmarks should look for discontinuous jumps, not just incremental improvements.

Section 9: Validation Roadmap

This is about testing the theory.

Collect detailed datasets: qubit metrics, coherence times, compiler efficiencies.

Apply change-point detection to see if real data fits the pattern.

Run pilot programs (labs, consortia) designed to intentionally trigger synergistic leaps.

Section 10: Policy and Strategy

Quantum computing is a geopolitical race.

Funding portfolios should balance safe bets with risky high-reward projects.

Standards and interoperability are crucial to allow breakthroughs to spread quickly.

International collaboration can accelerate progress but must balance security concerns.

Section 11: Broader Perspectives

Beyond the technical, sudden breakthroughs could have wide consequences:

Economics: Disruptions to cryptography, finance, and optimization.

Ethics: Researchers must communicate responsibly to avoid hype or panic.

Society: Governments and industries must prepare for sudden capability shocks.

Section 12: Conclusion

The conclusion restates the main idea: progress in quantum computing will come in irregular leaps, not smooth exponential growth. The (4, 16, 38, 139, ...) sequence provides a useful metaphor and model for this. Understanding and preparing for these jumps can help guide research, investment, and policy decisions.

Appendices

The appendices provide technical depth:

Mathematical derivations of recurrence relations and thresholds.

Simulation pseudocode for generating and testing the pattern.

Checklists for labs to track whether they're on a "pattern trajectory."

Research agenda for experiments, testbeds, and datasets.

Overall Message

The paper's core argument is that quantum computing breakthroughs are irregular, patterned, and catalyzed by threshold events. The sequence (4 → 16 → 38 → 139 → …) serves as a symbolic but structured way to think about those leaps. By embracing this lens, researchers, funders, and policymakers can better anticipate, prepare for, and even accelerate the arrival of quantum revolutions.

It's not just about numbers — it's about shaping expectations, designing better roadmaps, and avoiding blind reliance on smooth exponential forecasts.

Here's a long, expanded conclusion that draws out the insights of your paper and ties them together into a strong ending:

Expanded Conclusion: Insights from the Pattern-Based Perspective on Quantum Computing

The analysis presented in this paper has revolved around one central thesis: that the trajectory of quantum computing is not best understood as a smooth exponential curve, but rather as a series of punctuated, non-linear leaps. The sequence (4 → 16 → 38 → 139 → ...) is not merely a curiosity of mathematical growth but an interpretive framework that captures the texture of innovation in this field. By exploring its properties, mappings, and implications, we gain several important insights that deserve emphasis in conclusion.

1. Patterns as Predictive Lenses

One of the most valuable insights is that growth patterns provide a middle ground between deterministic laws (like Moore's Law) and chaotic unpredictability. The (4, 16, 38, 139, ...) sequence highlights the possibility of structured irregularity—progress that is not random but also not uniform. Recognizing such patterns allows us to forecast with humility: not by predicting exact dates or numbers, but by anticipating where to look for discontinuities and when to expect sudden accelerations.

2. Breakthroughs Are Catalytic, Not Incremental

Quantum computing progresses when diverse innovations align. A new material, a better control method, and a novel error-correcting code can interact to produce a leap that none of them could achieve individually. This is reflected in the pattern's jumps: they suggest that true breakthroughs are multiplicative, not additive. This insight should guide research strategy away from siloed optimization and toward cross-disciplinary integration.

3. Roadmaps Need Reframing

Most existing roadmaps track raw qubit counts or gate fidelities. While useful, these metrics mislead by suggesting that progress is steady. The pattern perspective suggests roadmaps should instead highlight milestones of effective capability: how many logical qubits, how many entangled nodes, or how deep a circuit can run. Reframing milestones in this way creates more realistic expectations and makes it easier to recognize when a true leap has occurred.

4. The Power of Nonlinear Scaling Laws

Mathematical models such as recurrence relations, percolation theory, and Bayesian change-point analysis demonstrate that irregular sequences can be formalized and studied rigorously. This insight matters because it bridges intuition with formalism: what looks like "messy, unpredictable progress" can in fact be modeled, tested, and even forecasted with the right tools. The contribution of this paper is therefore not just conceptual, but methodological—it provides concrete modeling approaches that future researchers can refine.

5. The Importance of Modularity and Interoperability

Architectural design choices—whether in superconducting qubits, trapped ions, photonic links, or hybrid systems—must be evaluated for their ability to catalyze breakthroughs. Modular systems that allow innovations in one part of the stack to ripple through the whole system are far more likely to produce pattern-like leaps. This highlights the deep insight that innovation is not just about advancing components, but about enabling combinations.

6. Algorithms as Hidden Multipliers

Another key takeaway is that breakthroughs are not confined to hardware. Algorithmic advances—better compilers, error-aware optimizations, hybrid methods—can unlock latent potential in hardware and trigger effective leaps. The insight here is that quantum advantage may arrive not from the biggest machine, but from the smartest integration of hardware and software.

7. Implications for Strategy and Policy

From a strategic perspective, this paper underscores that investment in quantum computing should not be treated like a smooth-growth trajectory. Instead, policymakers and funders should embrace uncertainty and allocate resources toward high-risk, high-reward initiatives capable of triggering leaps. International collaboration and the creation of interoperable standards can amplify the effect of breakthroughs when they occur, ensuring they are not isolated events but system-wide shifts.

8. Societal Readiness for Sudden Capability Jumps

Perhaps the most profound insight is that society at large must be ready for discontinuities. A sudden leap in quantum power could overturn cryptographic standards, reshape economic competitiveness, and accelerate discovery in fields ranging from chemistry to artificial intelligence. This requires ethical foresight and governance frameworks that can manage the consequences of abrupt technological discontinuities. Preparing for jumps is not only a technical necessity but a societal responsibility.

Final Reflection

The (4 → 16 → 38 → 139 → …) sequence is, at one level, a mathematical curiosity. But at a deeper level, it captures something essential about how revolutionary technologies unfold. Quantum computing, as one of the most consequential technologies of the 21st century, will likely not advance along smooth exponential curves but through the very kind of irregular, catalytic, pattern-driven leaps described here.

By recognizing this, we can design better experiments, fund smarter projects, and build more resilient policies. The sequence becomes more than numbers; it becomes a map of possibility, reminding us that the next great leap in quantum capability will not simply extend today's trajectory, but will emerge when unexpected alignments trigger transformative growth.

The core insight, therefore, is this: to shape the future of quantum computing, we must plan not for steady progress but for sudden breakthroughs—and the patterns that signal their approach.

Explanation of original paper

Here is a ~5-page style explanation (narrative summary plus critical commentary) of the original paper "Leveraging Growth Patterns for Innovation in Quantum …" (SSRN) — unpacking its arguments, contributions, strengths, and open questions.

Introduction & Context

The SSRN paper (titled Leveraging Growth Patterns for Innovation in Quantum …) proposes a bold rethinking of how we forecast and guide progress in quantum computing. Rather than assuming smooth exponential or logistic curves, the author suggests using discrete integer growth sequences (specifically the pattern 4 → 16 → 48 → 139, etc.) as a lens through which to understand breakthrough dynamics in quantum hardware, error correction, connectivity, and algorithms.

At its core, the paper reframes quantum computing's development trajectory as one driven by stepwise leaps, triggered when multiple sub-components (materials, control electronics, error codes, architecture, software) align. The unusual growth sequence is not claimed to be a literal "law," but rather a metaphorical and structural model to expose where and how discontinuities might arise.

The motivation is twofold:

1. Descriptive: Classical extrapolations (e.g. Moore's law analogues) fail to capture the empirical irregularity of progress in quantum systems.

2. Prescriptive: If we can see where leaps should be possible, we can better allocate research, funding, and architecture design to make them more likely.

By proposing the 4 → 16 → 48 → 139 pattern (which roughly accelerates in non-uniform increments), the paper seeks to map that pattern onto meaningful quantum metrics — logical qubits, error thresholds, interconnectivity, coherence improvements, algorithmic compression — and thereby offer a richer roadmap.

Key Arguments and Structure

1. The Growth Pattern as a Framing Device

The paper begins by arguing that the observed integer sequence (4, 16, 48, 139, …) captures certain qualitative features:

Irregular acceleration: The ratio between successive terms is not constant (16/4 = 4, 48/16 = 3, 139/48 ≈ 2.9).

Threshold-driven jumps: The idea is that after incremental improvements, some enabling technology or synergy triggers a disproportionately large jump.

Milestone notion: Rather than seeing the terms as every-state values, they represent milestones of effective capability: points where the system's performance or capacity shifts regime.

This treatment allows the author to break free from smooth continuous growth and instead think in terms of regimes, catalysts, and discontinuities.

2. Mapping to Quantum Layers

After setting up the pattern, the paper maps it to various layers of the quantum computing stack:

Qubit scaling & effective logical capacity: A key insight is that raw physical qubits are not the meaningful metric; what matters is the logical qubit (or usable effective capacity) after accounting for error correction, connectivity overhead, and noise. A jump in the pattern might correspond to a sudden drop in overhead or a new error-correction code enabling more efficient packing.

Error correction thresholds: Because fault-tolerant thresholds are highly nonlinear — a small improvement in gate fidelity or syndrome measurement overhead can dramatically reduce redundancy — the pattern can represent transitions in which a new code or concatenation strategy yields a leap in effective resource efficiency.

Entanglement / connectivity networks: The paper suggests that as hardware allows new coupler topologies or longer coherence links, network connectivity can cross percolation thresholds, causing the network to go from fragmented to richly connected. That percolation jump is well aligned with the discrete growth metaphor.

Coherence / gate fidelity: Advances in materials science, new qubit modalities, or better error suppression may permit jumps in coherence time or gate error rates sufficient to unlock deeper circuits or new algorithm classes.

Algorithmic & compiler improvements: The software side can act as a multiplier: optimization, circuit rewriting, error-aware compilation, or hybrid classical–quantum decomposition may serve as levers that convert hardware capability into effective quantum advantage in leaps.

By aligning each layer to a possible "jump point," the author shows that the pattern is not a childish numerology but a structured interpretive framework.

3. Modeling & Forecasting

One of the strengths of the paper is that it does not merely propose the metaphor, but builds modeling machinery to make it more precise:

Recurrence relations with shock terms: A model in which, where is a stochastic breakthrough term, is presented. The idea is that most of the time growth is multiplicative plus incremental, but occasionally a shock pushes you to a new regime.

Change-point / regime detection: To test whether real quantum progress aligns with discrete jumps, the author suggests using Bayesian change-point detection models: in effect, fitting data (qubit metrics, coherence, code performance) to a piecewise regime model rather than forcing a single smooth curve.

Simulation and synthetic experiments: The paper offers pseudocode and synthetic modeling to generate candidate sequences and test parameter settings (how frequent breakthroughs need to be, how large, how volatile) such that the early terms (4, 16, 48, 139) are reproduced or approximated.

Benchmarking & forecast uncertainty: Because of the scarcity of data in quantum computing (especially at regimes beyond current capability), the paper emphasizes that forecasts must come with wide uncertainty bounds and sensitivity analysis over model hyperparameters.

This modeling apparatus gives the paper more seriousness: it is not just speculative storytelling, but a framework that can be tested, falsified, or refined.

4. Case Studies and Plausible Scenarios

To ground the abstract in (semi) real examples, the paper sketches a few hypothetical or historically plausible analogues:

In superconducting qubits, a materials innovation or a new fabrication technique might suddenly reduce decoherence or crosstalk, causing a leap in usable qubits (i.e., you suddenly can lower error rates enough to cascade improvements).

In trapped-ion architectures, adoption of new interconnect schemes or multi-zone shuttling might allow scaling that was previously infeasible, triggering a jump in connectivity.

For emerging topological qubits, a working demonstration of non-abelian anyons or Majorana-like states may represent a huge jump: the transition from hypothetical to stable physical qubits could map to a step in the pattern.

The paper also alludes to hybrid systems (mixing platforms) or catalytic integration (e.g., combining photonics with superconducting control) as potential jump catalysts.

While these are speculative, they serve the role of bridging mathematical metaphor to engineering reality.

5. Implications & Strategy

Finally, the author draws out a variety of implications:

Roadmap design: Instead of targeting smooth continuous progress (e.g. "double qubits every 18 months"), roadmaps should define milestone regimes — points at which effective capability leaps.

Funding strategy: A portion of funding should be reserved for high-risk, high-leverage projects whose returns might trigger a jump (rather than all funds going to incremental extension).

Modularity & interoperability: Systems should be designed so breakthroughs in one component (say, error correction) can propagate to the rest of the stack — increasing the chance that disparate gains align to form a jump.

International cooperation vs competition: Because the impact of a leap in quantum power is globally significant (cryptography, materials discovery, optimization), cooperation in testbeds and standards may help accelerate leaps; but strategic competition may push secrecy and fragmentation.

Governance and ethical readiness: Sudden leaps in capability carry risks (e.g. cryptographic breakage) and demand readiness in policy, public communication, and oversight.

Contributions and Novel Insights

This SSRN paper offers several contributions and fresh perspectives:

1. A new forecasting metaphor. Rather than defaulting to exponentials or logistic models, the use of an irregular integer sequence opens the door to thinking about innovative discontinuities.

2. Layered mapping. The paper does not restrict itself to qubit counts; it covers error correction, connectivity, coherence, and software, showing that leaps can emerge at multiple levels.

3. Testable modeling frameworks. The use of recurrence + shock models, Bayesian change-point techniques, and simulation gives the metaphor rigor and opens possibilities for empirical validation.

4. Strategic guidance. The leap-aware perspective yields concrete suggestions for roadmap design, funding allocation, architectural modularity, and governance.

5. Bridging metaphor and mechanism. The author does not leave the pattern abstract; instead, they actively explore how engineering or algorithmic breakthroughs plausibly instantiate the pattern.

Critiques, Challenges & Open Questions

No proposal is without challenges. Here are some critical perspectives and open issues the paper leaves partly unresolved:

Data sparsity / calibration risk: The quantum field is still early. We have few reliable historical data points to calibrate a discrete-leap model. It's possible that fitting a weird integer pattern is overfitting on weak signals.

Sequence uniqueness / arbitrariness: Why exactly 4 → 16 → 48 → 139 and not another sequence? The choice risks appearing ad hoc. The metaphorical power is strong, but its empirical grounding is weaker.

Alignment uncertainties: Mapping a sequence term to a real quantum metric — e.g. saying "this term corresponds to a new error-correction capability" — may be ambiguous and subjective. There may be multiple plausible interpretations for a jump.

Predictive failure risk: If a leap doesn't arrive at the predicted milestone, the model could be falsified or lose credibility. The author must plan for negative results.

Non-unique leap paths: There may be more than one way to jump; parallel architectures may diverge. A discrete-sequence model may oversimplify a branching horizon of possibilities.

Policy latency: Even when a leap is imminent, policy, regulation, standardization, and industry adoption may lag, muting the impact of the leap.

Despite these challenges, the paper doesn't pretend its model is perfect — rather it proposes a framing for deeper exploration.

How to Read This Paper in Practice

If you (as a researcher, funder, or architect) take this paper seriously, here is how to engage with it:

1. Collect metric time-series: Track physical qubit counts, logical qubit counts (post-error-correction), coherence times, gate fidelities, connectivity graphs, and software compression ratios.

2. Fit models to data: Compare the jump-driven recurrence models against conventional exponential models. Use Bayesian change-point tools to see whether regime shifts are detectable.

3. Design experiments for catalysts: Establish pilot testbeds that combine improvements in materials, control electronics, and code designs simultaneously, to amplify the chance of synergistic leaps.

4. Define milestone regimes: In your roadmap, label certain "jump targets" (e.g. "achieve logical qubits > 50 with overhead ratio < 50x") rather than projecting only smooth curves.

5. Risk management: Carry parallel fallback trajectories. If a leap fails, learn from failure. If it happens early, be ready to scale quickly.

Final Reflection

The SSRN paper challenges the conventional wisdom that quantum computing will evolve in smooth, predictable curves. Instead, it frames progress as punctuated, regime-shifting, and synergy-driven — with the 4 → 16 → 48 → 139 pattern serving as a provocative but meaningful lens.

Its strength lies in combining metaphor with modeling, across hardware, error correction, connectivity, and software. It invites the community to shift from linear extrapolation to leap-based thinking. While its empirical calibration is uncertain and many mapping choices are speculative, the value lies in reshaping how we think about progress, risk, roadmap design, and strategic funding in quantum computing.

www.ingramcontent.com/pod-product-compliance
Lightning Source LLC
La Vergne TN
LVHW022323200926
848481LV00004B/1405